SERMON OUTLINES FOR FUNERALS

SERMON OUTLINES FOR FUNERALS

C. W. Keiningham

BAKER BOOK HOUSE
Grand Rapids, Michigan 49506

a division of Baker Publishing Group
P.O. Box 6287, Grand Rapids, MI 49516-6287
www.bakerbooks.com

ISBN 10: 0-8010-5427-3
ISBN 978-0-8010-5427-3

Seventeenth printing, August 2006

Printed in the United States of America

Contents

SERMON OUTLINES FOR FUNERALS

1
Seed of Abraham

Genesis 25:8

I. God's Call Was the Beginning — Genesis 12:1
- A. God's call is the beginning of real life
- B. God's call is to everyone — Matt. 24:18-20

II. God's Justification Is by Believing — Rom. 4:3
- A. "Righteousness" means attained right-standing
- B. Righteousness can be attained
  1. Not by works of righteousness — Titus 3:5
  2. Not by religious activity — Matt. 6:7
  3. By believing — Rom. 4:3

III. God's Call Is Obeyed by Faith — Heb. 11:8
- A. To receive a call is not enough
  1. Mother who gets no response when she calls her child
- B. God's call requires a response
  1. Faith is proven by obedience
  2. Faith without works is dead — James 2:17

IV. God's Friendship Was Enjoyed — James 2:23
- A. This is a blessed part of being a Christian
- B. God's friendship was enjoyed in good times and bad

V. God's Dwelling Place Was Sought — Heb. 11:10
- A. Abraham lived 175 years but the world was never his home
- B. Abraham knew he had a home not built with hands
- C. So it is with every Christian

VI. Abraham Went to Be with the Lord — Matt. 22:32
- A. To say he died is not sufficient
- B. To have that hope for Abraham is to have the same hope for the deceased

2

Poor Person

I Kings 8:18-19

1. By what criteria do we judge the success of a life?
   a. Length of years or accomplishments?
2. Two things testify to the value of a life

I. Personal Ambitions

A. We don't always achieve our dreams
   1. That doesn't make them valueless — v. 18

B. Unfulfilled dreams provide several lessons
   1. The incompleteness of earthly life
      a. Abraham sought a city but got a grave
      b. Moses led the quest but never entered the promised land
   2. The inherent rightness of God's sovereignty
      a. God decided David would die before the temple was built
      b. David's devotion — no murmuring

C. There is value in unfulfilled dreams
   1. God was pleased with David — v. 18b
   2. Solomon was challenged and inspired

II. Personal Relationship with God

A. Right with God means right in life
   1. Life is not given to be wasted
   2. Life is futile unless we are right with God
      a. Right with His purpose and aim
      b. Right with His attitude and position
   3. Must be able to say with Paul — Phil. 3:13-14

B. How does one get right with God?
   1. Acknowledge and renounce sin
   2. Receive Jesus as Savior — Rom. 10:13

3
A Precious Life

Job 28:10b

1. Many things in life are precious to us
   a. We try to protect ourselves and our property with insurance, locks, alarms, and banks
2. The most precious things are relationships
   a. Relationships to people are precious
      (1) Death becomes a heart-rending intruder
   b. Relationship to the church is special
   c. Relationship to God is the most precious one we can have
3. Many things also are precious to God (text) — Ps. 116:15

I. Speaks of God's Feelings for His Children
- A. Bible assures us of God's love — Rom. 5:8; 8:35-39
- B. This assurance gives us strength in life
  1. In times of trouble, strife, and sorrow
- C. This assurance gives us confidence in death

II. Speaks of God's Provision for His Children
- A. We don't know much about what happens after death
- B. We know only what the Bible tells us
  1. We know it is not the end of life
     a. Death of the body is a transition
  2. We know His children have a place prepared for them — John 14
  3. We know someday we shall receive our bodies

III. Speaks of God's Action at the Death of His Children
- A. Can we imagine that God stood by and did nothing?
- B. If there were a fire in our church, we would want to do something. The building is special to us.
  1. Surely God acts to help in our hour of need
  2. We are precious in His sight

4

In the Shepherd's Cave

Psalm 23

1. Millions know and love this psalm
   a. The words inspire, instruct, and comfort

I. He Speaks of a Relationship with God — v. 1a

A. He was saying, "I belong to God"
   1. We might say, "Jesus is Lord"
   2. Both mean we are children of God

B. He was just a common man
   1. This says that a relationship is possible for any person
   2. It is possible for anyone to be a Christian — II Peter 3:9

II. He Speaks of a Relationship in Life

A. How the relationship touched his life
   1. Physical needs met — "not want"
   2. Emotional needs met — "still waters"
   3. Spiritual needs met — "restoreth soul"
   4. Living needs met — "paths of righteousness"
   5. Deepest needs met — "shadow of death"
   6. Total needs met — "table before me"

B. The relationship was not temporary — v. 6

III. He Speaks of an Eternal Relationship

A. Eternal dwelling place —v. 6b

B. Eternal well-being — v. 6a

C. This is a possibility for all who believe

D. Who of us can say, "The Lord is my shepherd"?

5
Drawing Near to God

Psalm 73:3, 25-28

1. The psalmist was confirming his faith
   a. It seemed as if the wicked prospered and the good died young
   b. God revealed the truth to him — Ps. 119:155

I. Good Comes to Those Who Draw Near
   A. God will draw near to them — James 4:8-10
      1. God wants to move in permanently
      2. All Satan's efforts aim at preventing closeness to God
   B. We will know God's will — II Peter 1:21
   C. We will be able to pray and serve better
      1. Both depend on closeness to God
   D. We will enjoy closer fellowship — II Thess. 1:3
   E. We will have greater joy in service — Ps. 122:1
   F. We will have greater peace in trouble — Ps. 27:1
      1. When death invades our circle of dear ones
      2. When sorrow floods our souls

II. It Is Possible to Draw Near to God
   A. When our hearts and spirits are wounded
      1. The Lord is near — Ps. 34:18
      2. This is when we need to draw near
      3. This is when we are inclined to draw near
   B. When our future seems uncertain — John 14:6
      1. In the confusion of life there is a way
      2. In the deception of life there is truth
      3. In the conclusion of life there is life
   C. It is good to trust in the Lord

6

Deep Thoughts

Psalm 94:17-19

1. Note the psalmist's circumstances and thoughts
2. Today we have mixed emotions and thoughts

I. Thoughts of Sorrow

A. Grief and melancholy

B. Another chapter in our book is over

II. Thoughts of Comfort

A. Death brings a feeling of defeat

B. The Christian believes that death is a triumph — Col.2:15

III. Thoughts of Love

A. These are intensified at death

B. Thoughts of God's love — John 3:16

IV. Thoughts of Eternity

A. Death and what lies beyond mystifies us

B. Death turns our thoughts to eternity

1. Impresses on us the need to prepare
2. Inspires us to do some "repairing"

V. Thoughts of Concern

A. Concern for family members

1. We should be concerned at all times
2. The Bible says people without Christ are lost

VI. Thoughts of Disappointment

A. We mull over what we should have said or done

B. This should encourage us to act now to improve our personal relationships with friends and family

VII. Thoughts of Gratitude

A. For the blessings of God

B. For the advantages of our lives

C. For the privilege of our relationships

7
Looking for Help

Psalm 121:1

1. Many experiences cause fear and concern
2. Many ask, "Where can I turn?"

I. Look Up — His Overshadowing Wings — Ps. 91:4
- A. We don't always look in the right places
- B. We look to God and find Him sufficient
  1. Ruth 2:12; II Cor. 12:9

II. Look Down — His Everlasting Arms — Deut. 33:27a
- A. Peter looked down and saw waves — Matt. 14:30
- B. Faith sees God's strong arms
  1. Children of Israel — Ps. 77:15
  2. Jesus and children — Mark 10:16
  3. We are His children — Matt. 10:28-31

III. Look Around — His Encamping Angels — Ps. 34:7
- A. This was a testimony of personal experience
  1. David and Goliath — I Sam. 17:32-37
- B. Many others could also testify
  1. Elisha and servant — II Kings 6:15-18
  2. Daniel — Dan. 6:22
  3. Peter in prison — Acts 5:19

IV. Look Inside — His Peace — Phil. 4:7
- A. This is the only place some have to look for help
  1. "The only thing we have to fear is fear itself"(FDR)
  2. Let God's peace rule — Col. 3:15
- B. May the Lord give you peace today — II Thess. 3:16.

8

The Gift of Sleep

Psalm 127:2

I. They Are Called "His Beloved"

A. God loves all people
1. Some say, "But I'm so bad"
2. See I Tim. 1:15; Rom. 5:8; John 3:16

B. Some occupy a special place in God's affection
1. "Beloved" is used to describe Jesus
2. Beloved of God occupy a similar place
a. They are sons — John 1:12; I John 3:1-2
b. They are heirs — Rom. 8:15-17; Gal. 4:7
c. They are His by special ties
(1) By purchase — I Peter 1:18-19
(2) By adoption — Rom. 8:15
(3) In obedience — John 14:21

II. They Are Given Sleep

A. The psalm speaks of rest and satisfaction
1. In regard to cares of world
2. In regard to sin

B. Speaks of a temporary condition
1. Jairus' daughter — Mark 5:39
2. Paul speaks of the dead as being asleep — I Thess. 4:15-16

C. Speaks of a permanent condition — Rev. 21:3-5

III. Let Us Take This to Heart

A. A lesson in the midst of sorrow
1. It is important to prepare
2. It is important to live close to God

9
Good Woman

Proverbs 31:10-31

1. The worth of a good woman — v. 10

I. Her Inestimable Value

A. More valuable than material things — v.10b

1. The value of a soul — Matt. 16:26

B. Valuable because she is industrious — vv. 13, 14, 16, 19, 21

C. Valuable because she is devoted — vv. 12, 15

D. Valuable because she is compassionate — v. 20

1. Judgment day — Matt. 25:31-46

E. Valuable because of her character — vv. 11, 25

II. Her Family's Estimate of Her

A. Children call her blessed — v. 28a

B. Husband praises her — v. 28b

C. Community honors her by honoring her husband — v. 23

D. Of 22 verses, 13 begin with "she"

1. This places emphasis on the woman herself
2. Matthew Henry said this portrait is a mirror for all women to look into.

III. Her Ultimate Worth Lies in Her Godliness — vv. 29-30

A. Certain things are responsible for her faith

1. Church attendance and spiritual nourishment through the Word
2. Involvement in serving God and man
3. Time spent in prayer and meditation

B. Such faith is possible for all

IV. One Last Observation

A. She shall rejoice in the future — v. 25

B. No doubt the deceased is rejoicing today — Rev. 21:2-7

10

Hope for a Sinner

Nahum 1:7

1. The text tells us that the Lord is good
   a. We sometimes feel that nothing is good
      (1) Because of social ills and human wickedness
      (2) Because of disappointment in people
      (3) Because of disappointment in ourselves
2. God's Word gives us hope in life

I. He Shows His Goodness by His Concern

A. Not willing that any should perish — II Peter 3:9
   1. The psalmist said: "No man cared . . ." — Ps. 142:4
   2. Jesus said: "Not one (sparrow) . . ." — Matt. 10:29
   3. Jesus said: "Hairs . . . numbered" — Matt. 10:30

II. He Shows His Goodness by His Mercy

A. Prodigal son illustrates a father's mercy — Luke 15:11-24
   1. The father's love reached into far country
   2. All of us have strayed like sheep — Isa. 53:6
   3. A cry for forgiveness never goes unheard
      a. Publican — Luke 18:13; Thief — Luke 23:42

B. None of us is beyond God's mercy

III. He Shows His Goodness by His Willingness to Receive

A. "I will in no wise cast out" — John 6:37

B. "Draw nigh to God, and he will draw nigh to you" — James 4:8

C. "He knoweth them that trust" (text)
   1. To know you belong to God is a source of comfort and strength
   2. Our life and death are in our own hands — Rev. 3:20

11
Life's Values

Matthew 4:1-4

I. We Are Tempted to Misplace Our Values
- A. Our physical needs are very real
  - 1. A baby cries to communicate its physical needs
- B. Physical needs can become a consuming passion
  - 1. Smother spiritual needs — Matt. 13:22
  - 2. Displace God's will — Prodigal son
- C. This was the temptation of Jesus (text)
- D. This is the temptation of every person

II. We Are Encouraged to Rightly Place Our Values
- A. Life is more than the body — the physical
  - 1. This is our hope in death
  - 2. This is what Jesus was saying — Matt. 6:25
- B. Life is primarily spiritual
  - 1. Jesus often emphasized this — Matt. 6:33
    - a. Story of rich farmer — Luke 12:16-20
  - 2. The body dies but the soul lives on
- C. So we are to "set" our "affections on things above"

III. We Should Value Our Relationship to God Above All
- A. Above our physical well-being
  - 1. Apostles could have avoided danger by compromising
  - 2. Being true to God is more important than life
- B. In this hour we are being tempted
  - 1. To think of physical aspects of death rather than spiritual
    - a. We mourn the physical absence of our loved one
    - b. We should be cheered by the spiritual release of our loved one
- C. In this hour, we think of our relationship to God

12

Mother

Matthew 8:14-15

I. Every Mother Has a Twofold Duty in Life

A. Submit to the Savior

1. Means accepting Him as Savior
2. Means obeying His commands

B. Minister to her family members

1. Requires being alert and able
2. Requires being willing

II. A Mother's Ministry Is Sometimes Interrupted

A. Death is always sad

1. Peter's family was sad (text)
2. We are sad as we say farewell
   a. The family mourns a loss

B. Things besides death can interrupt

1. Sin and worldly pursuits

III. The Difference in the Text from Today

A. Peter's mother-in-law got well

1. God chose to heal her

B. In our case, the mother didn't get well — Isa. 55:8-9; Rom. 11:33

1. Why would God choose not to heal?
   a. See Prov. 14:12-13
   b. Perhaps He had something better for her — Rev. 19:4-9; 21:9-14; 22:1-5
2. Death is part of our inheritance — Ps. 127:2
3. Imagine what she saw when she crossed over to eternal life

13
Burden Bearer

Matthew 11:28

I. The Problem — Labored and Heavy Laden
  A. Some are burdened with distresses
    1. Poverty, temptation, sickness, etc.
  B. Some are burdened with sorrow
    1. Jesus understands — Isa. 53:3
  C. Some are oppressed with sin
    1. People bear no greater burden
  C. To all of these Jesus addresses Himself

II. The Promise — "I Will Give You Rest"
  A. Jesus offers rest for body and soul
    1. To the weary, anxious, and bewildered
  B. Jesus offers pardon for the sinful
    1. Rest for conscience and heart — grace
  C. Jesus offers rest with God in heaven — Rev. 21:1-5

III. The Proposition — "Come Unto Me"
  A. Indicates to whom we are to come
    1. We can go many places and not find rest
    2. Jesus is the Rock
  B. Indicates some action on our part
    1. The Prodigal Son acted — Luke 15:18-20
    2. The demoniac came to Jesus — Mark 5:6

IV. The Persons — All Ye
  A. God's love extends to all
    1. No matter how sinful we are or how often we have rejected Christ
    2. No one must cross Jordan alone
  B. God's grace is offered to all
  C. God's rest is offered to all

14

Son

Luke 7:11-16

1. Note woman's circumstances, plans, and despair
2. One came who would change her life

I. Jesus Saw and Had Compassion

A. The Lord is not unmindful of suffering
  1. What He saw that touched Him
    a. The mother was weeping
      (1) Loss of a child is especially touching
      (2) David's lament over Absalom — II Sam. 18:33
    b. The deceased was a young man and the widow's only son

B. The Lord is not unfeeling toward human suffering
  1. "Compassion" means felt her sorrow

C. Faith in His compassion is our hope
  1. How else can we hope for salvation?
  2. How else can we expect sustenance?
  3. How else can we look for resurrection?

II. Jesus Said, "Weep Not"

A. Two reasons Jesus can put away sorrow
  1. He puts away the cause, sin, which is the root of all misery
  2. He has all power, even over death — I Thess. 4:13-18

III. Jesus Said, "Arise"

A. What a change this one word wrought
  1. Death was swallowed up in victory
  2. The young man was restored to his mother
  3. The widow went her way rejoicing

B. There will be rejoicing in this family again

15
Birth and Death

John 3:18

1. Proposition: He who is born once dies twice. He who is born twice dies once.

I. 'Born Once' Refers to Physical Birth
- A. Everyone dies once and is born once
- B. Man and God do not see eye to eye — Isa. 55
  1. Sin has distorted man's vision
  2. Man rejoices at birth and mourns at death
  3. Man should rejoice at death

II. 'Dies Twice' Refers to Death of Body and Soul
- A. All men die physically — Heb. 9:27
  1. This is the death that none can escape
- B. There is another death for those who are 'born once'
  1. It is called "second death" — Rev. 20:11-15
  2. It is forever and irreversible
- C. The victims of this second death
  1. Those whose names are not in the book of life
     - a. Physical births are recorded in court records
     - b. Spiritual births are recorded in heaven

III. 'Born Twice' Refers to Spiritual Birth
- A. The second birth is a necessity — John 3:3
- B. The second birth distinguishes the "Christian"
- C. The twice-born person has had a life-changing experience
  1. Realized his lost condition
  2. Repented and believed on Jesus

IV. 'Dies Once' Refers to Physical Death
- A. The names of the saved are written in the book of life
- B. The saved are excused from the second death
  1. Because of what Jesus did on the cross
  2. Because of their faith in Jesus

16

Church Member

John 10:27-30

1. People have always believed in life after death
   a. Earliest man buried weapons with the deceased
   b. Indians were said to bury a brave on his horse
   c. Pharaoh's treasure and slaves were buried with him
2. People have always longed for eternal life
   a. Explorers sought the "Fountain of Youth"
   b. Science explores the secrets of life
3. Jesus promised eternal life to those who believe

I. How Does One Come to Have Eternal Life?

A. Not by simply believing in God — James 2:19

B. Not by belonging to some church

C. Not by observing religious rituals

D. Jesus pointed to Himself — John 11:25

1. Life is imparted by the person of Jesus — John 10:28
2. Jesus said: "He that believeth in me"
   a. Belief is not merely approval
   b. Belief is trusting Him more than anything else

II. We Have Every Hope for the Deceased

A. Not because of certain externals

1. Not because the person was a church member
2. Not because the person observed rites and rituals

B. Because the person's trust was in the person of Jesus

17
Jesus and Death

John 13:1

1. People often wish they could speak to the deceased just one more time
2. Preachers would also like to speak to them once more
3. The best we can do now is for me to speak to you
4. Let me speak of eternal things

I. Jesus Knew Death Was Near
- A. He did not think of death as final
  1. He was departing from this world
  2. He was going to a better world
- B. We know death is near to all of us
  1. Our "days are as grass" — Ps. 103:15
  2. We begin to die the minute we are born
- C. We don't know the exact day or hour
  1. The summons often comes abruptly

II. Jesus Knew Where He Was Going
- A. Do you know where you are going?
- B. Every Christian has been told — John 14:2-3

III. How Does One Become a Child of God?
- A. By receiving Jesus as Savior — John 1:12; Rev. 3:20
- B. The invitation is extended to all — John 7:37

IV. Jesus Loved Them to the End
- A. Savior's love for His own never fails
  1. When we need salvation
  2. When we need strength
  3. When we face death
- B. Death is not to be feared — Rom. 8:35-39

18

The Greatest Promise

John 14:1-3

1. This was the greatest promise ever made because. . .

I. Made by the Greatest Person Who Ever Lived

A. Jesus' life determined the course of history

B. His life was totally unselfish — Phil. 2:5-8

II. About the Greatest Place Ever Imagined

"In my Father's house are many mansions"

A. Man's greatest efforts are hovels in comparison

B. Description — Rev. 21:10-23

III. Its Purpose Is Our Eternal Comfort

A. Provides comfort now — "Let not your heart be troubled"

B. Provides comfort after death — "I go to prepare"

C. No more sorrow, pain, or death

IV. Rests on Greatest Proposition

"Believe in God . . .believe in me"

A. This proposition is called the "grace of God"

B. It is a promise to all who believe

V. Required Greatest of Preparation

Galatians 4:4: "But when the fulness of the time was come, God sent forth his Son . . ."

A. "Fulness" refers to preparation on earth

B. Jesus had to live, die, rise from the dead, and ascend

VI. Holds Forth Greatest Prospect

"I will come again, and receive you"

A. Prospect for the living and the dead

B. Paul's verification — I Thess. 4:15-18

C. We have no reason to doubt —"If it were not so, I would have told you"

19
Peace of God

John 14:27

1. Henry Van Dyke: "(Peace) is reward of righteous, the blessing of good, crown of life's effort and the glory of eternity."
2. Peace fortifies us to face life's experiences
   a. It is sufficient even in time of death — Phil. 4:11-13

I. It Is the Peace of Being Divinely Loved

A. Nothing satisfies like being loved
   1. No love satisfies like God's love
   2. A daughter was listening to the beating of her mother's heart. "What is that?" "Love" "What is love?" "Look into my eyes. What do you see?" "A little girl" "Who?" "Me" "That's love. That's what is in my heart."

B. God's great love is revealed in Christ — I John 4:9-10
   1. Christ is our source of strength
   2. Christ is our source of comfort
   3. Christ is our source of peace

II. It Is the Peace of Being Divinely Controlled

A. Imagine erecting a building with no design!

B. It is what many are doing with their life — Isa. 53:6

C. If we accept God's design for life, we have peace

III. It Is the Peace of Being Divinely Forgiven

A. Sin causes unrest within
   1. It is like the vexation of an unresolved problem

B. There is rest and peace in Christ
   1. There is forgiveness through Him — Acts 5:31; 13:38
   2. Christian peace is provided through forgiveness of sins
   3. This peace is available to all

20

Christian Woman

Acts 9:36-42; Revelation 14:13

1. Parallel between the deceased and Dorcas

I. Both Were Disciples of Jesus Christ

A. This means they believed certain things

1. The claims of Jesus about Himself
2. The death of Jesus was for their own sin

B. This means they acted on those beliefs

II. Both Proved Their Position by Actions

A. They were full of good works

1. Works of charity and benevolence
2. Aid to the needy — James 2:14-17

B. They had witnesses to their character

1. Witness of family and friends — v. 39
2. Witness of heaven itself — II Tim. 4:8

III. Both Were Removed in Midst of Usefulness

A. None of us will escape death

1. It is appointed — Heb. 9:27

B. Death does not end our usefulness

1. Their influence continues even today

IV. Both Had a Preacher Called in to Minister

A. All that could be done was done for both

B. God gives the minister a small garden to tend. In it are many flowers. One beautiful flower God stooped and plucked for Himself. "This deserves a better place and better care." With God the flower will grow forever and become more beautiful.

1. We don't begrudge the empty space in the garden
2. We are thankful we had such a rose for a while

21
A Time of Parting

Acts 20:36-38

1. Paul was just completing his second missionary journey
2. Paul called the elders of Ephesus together to encourage them
3. Goodbyes are always moving experiences

I. A Time of Sorrow
- A. Because they would "see his face no more"
  - 1. Death is a similar experience
- B. Because of the effect Paul had on their lives
  - 1. Introduced them to Jesus and nurtured their faith
  - 2. Watched over them and instructed them
- C. Their sorrow was openly expressed — v. 37
  - 1. Weeping is language understood by all
  - 2. Our Lord wept often — John 11

II. A Time of Separation
- A. Paul was leaving them for the last time
  - 1. Paul had sensed the finality of it
  - 2. Dying saints often sense the coming separation
- B. They stayed with Paul to the very end
  - 1. They accompanied him to the ship — v. 38b
  - 2. Family and friends stay with the loved one to the end

III. A Time of Victory
- A. They realized they would see Paul again
  - 1. At the coming of the Lord — I Thess. 4:13-18
- B. Victory does not lie in circumstances
  - 1. It rests in the will of God
  - 2. John the Baptist was a victor in death
  - 3. Paul and Silas were victors in jail
- C. Victory rests in the person of Jesus Christ — I Cor. 15:55-57

22

Staggering at Promises

Romans 4:13, 18-25

I. John 11:25

A. "If a man die, shall he live again?" — Job 14:14
  1. Science tells us, "No, he shall not."
  2. Experience tells us, "No, he shall not."

B. The Word of God says, "Yes, he shall!"
  1. Jesus to Martha — John 11:23-26
  2. All things are possible — Mark 9:23

II. John 3:16

A. Church membership means little after death

B. Knowing Jesus as Savior means everything — John 14:6

C. Many stagger at this promise
  1. Rich young ruler — Matt. 19:16-22
  2. Hard for some to accept — Eph. 2:8, 9
  3. Paul to Judaizers — Gal. 3:24-26

III. I Thessalonians 4:16-18

A. Men of every age have doubted the return of Christ
  1. Biblical days — II Peter 3:4
  2. Today many people don't look for His coming

B. Christians look for His appearing
  1. They believe His return will be just as the Bible says
    a. With a shout, the voice of the archangel, and the trump of God
    b. "Lazarus, come forth" — John 11:43
    c. Isaiah 60:1
  2. The dead in Christ will rise first
  3. The living in Christ will catch up with them
  4. All of us will be with the Lord forever

C. Comfort one another with these words

23

Two Kinds of Servants

Romans 6:16-23

1. Solemn pronouncement — Rev. 22:11

I. Two Kinds of Life Set Forth

- A. No alternate ways are set forth
  - 1. Everyone is living one way or the other
- B. Life of service to sin
  - 1. Sin is transgression of the law — John 3:4
  - 2. Two great commandments — Matt. 22:37-40
- C. Life of service to Christ
  - 1. One who follows, serves, and obeys Christ
  - 2. One who loves the divine Word and presence

II. Two Destinies of Man Set Forth

- A. Again there are no alternates
  - 1. Every person can count on one or the other
- B. The destiny of servants of sin — vv. 21, 23
  - 1. Parable of the barren fig tree — Luke 13:6-9
  - 2. God is not mocked — Gal. 6:7
- C. The destiny of servants of Christ
  - 1. Gift of God is eternal life — v. 23b
    - a. The nature of the gift — free
    - b. The source of the gift — God
  - 2. "Life" means consciousness, existence, satisfaction
  - 3. This life offered to all — Rev. 22:17
    - a. Promise is through Jesus Christ — v. 23
    - b. Received as Christ is received — I John 5:12

24

Dealing with God

Romans 10:8-13

1. All must deal with the same God
2. We have some encouragement — v. 12b
3. Some things never change

I. Human Nature

A. Our greatest struggles are with our own human nature

B. There is comfort — the war is over — Rom. 7:23-25

II. God's Character

A. Mal. 3:6a can be a comfort or a threat

B. Four aspects of character that never change

1. Sovereignty — "I am the Lord"
   a. As Lord, He has the final say
2. Justice — Deut. 32:4
   a. God cannot be unfair; He is just
3. Love — I John 4:8
   a. Exercising love has some limitations
   b. "God is love" and has no limitations
4. Mercy — Ps. 136 (all 26 verses end the same)
   a. God's love follows from cradle to grave and beyond

III. God's Word

A. It shall stand forever — Isa. 40:8

B. The unchanging Word is a source of strength and comfort

1. "I will give you rest" — Matt. 11:28
2. "I will in no wise cast out" — John 6:37
3. Whatever your need today, come to Jesus

25

"God Is Love"

Romans 15:1-5; I John 4:8

1. Misconceptions of God are common
   a. After WWI man portrayed God as an angry, vengeful God
   b. Many think of God as a tyrant trying to yoke mankind
2. I John 4:8 is a comforting description of God
3. Shakespeare: "They have not loved who do not show their love."

I. God Shows Love by Providing for Our Salvation

A. Humans do not deserve salvation

B. In spite of this, God loves us

1. So much that He sent His Son — John 3:16
2. So much that He established the church as a guiding light
3. So much that He is willing to forgive the vilest of sinners

II. God Shows Love by Providing for Our Sustenance

A. In hours of temptation and affliction

1. God released Paul and Silas from jail — Acts 16:16-40
2. Paul learned to be content — Phil. 4:11

B. In hours of sorrow and sadness

1. In the "valley of the shadow of death" — Ps. 23
2. In Israel's affliction God was afflicted — Isa. 63:9
3. It is hard to believe, but God understands our feelings
   a. An artist was teaching a boy to draw. The boy became discouraged at his lack of progress. The artist encouraged him by saying, "You draw as good as I did when I was your age."
   b. The Word became flesh, suffered and died

C. A man tried to wipe frost from a window in order to see out

1. A friend said, "Let me light a fire and it will melt."
2. God says, "Let my love come in and the frost will melt away."

26

Sufferer

II Corinthians 4:8-18

I. No One Is Excluded from Suffering

A. This causes disillusionment with Christianity

1. Christians experience persecution — II Tim. 3:12

B. We know that the best of people suffer

1. Prophecy concerning Paul — Acts 9:16
2. All apostles but John suffered martyrdom

C. At times Christians become dejected — v.9

1. Christians do not despair — vv. 8-9

II. The Christian Is Renewed in Suffering — v.16

A. Several reasons Christians do not faint

1. We have the spirit of faith
2. We have the hope of resurrection

B. This can be every Christian's testimony

1. We must maintain fellowship with God
2. We must do several things to maintain fellowship
   a. Regular prayer and Bible study
   b. Regular worship and fellowship
3. We can have victory — I Cor. 15:57

III. A Word to Non-Christians

A. Death is inevitable for every person

1. Scripture and experience confirm this
2. The service today reminds us of this

B. Death need not be a defeat

1. Christ won the victory for us on the cross
2. Victory was assured by the resurrection
3. There is hope for all through Jesus Christ

27

Death -- Friend or Foe?

II Corinthians 5:8-10

1. Paul spoke of the two bodies of the saints
   a. The present or earthly body — mortal
   b. The future or heavenly body — eternal
2. Death is laying one body down and taking up the other

I. Death Doesn't Endanger a Christian's Interests

A. Everyone has investments in life
   1. The investments of some are in this life
      a. They depend on our presence here
      b. Death endangers these investments
   2. The investments of a Christian are in heaven — Col. 3:2
B. Death has a profitable effect for a Christian
   1. Allows him to claim his interest
C. Christians have a different state of mind — II Cor. 5:8
   1. This is not a natural attitude toward death
   2. This is not saying we wish to die

II. Death Doesn't Destroy a Christian's Purpose

A. Every person has a purpose in life
   1. This purpose gives value to life
   2. Death can be a threat, depending on life's purpose
B. Christian purpose — II Cor. 5:9
C. The Christian purpose is not destroyed by death

III. Death Doesn't Prevent a Christian's Rewards

A. Every person seeks rewards in life
   1. To the worldly, the rewards are in this life
      a. Death prevents them from collecting
   2. Christian rewards are in the future life
      a. Death expedites the collecting of rewards — I Peter 1:3-4
B. The Christian's rewards are in heaven

28

Redeemer

I Thessalonians 4:13-18

1. We are reminded constantly of the nearness of death
2. Death has different meaning to different people

I. Think About the Redeemed of God

A. All mankind has been sold into sin
   1. Because of Adam, the human race is under the power of sin — Rom. 5:12

B. Jesus came and bought us back — I Peter 1:18
   1. God made a deal (covenant) with His Son

II. Think About the Death of the Redeemed

A. Death is compared to sleep
   1. Sleep is an interval between activities

B. It is referred to as "departing" — Phil. 1:23

C. It is thought of as a change of residence — John 14

D. It is considered a gain — Phil. 1:21

III. Think About the Destiny of the Redeemed

A. What happens to the body of the redeemed?
   1. It is buried to await resurrection

B. What happens to the soul of the redeemed?
   1. Jesus' promise to the thief — Luke 23:43
   2. "Absent from body . . . present with the Lord — II Cor. 5:8

C. Eventually body and soul will be reunited

IV. Think About Us Here Today

A. Some of us are the redeemed
   1. The hope expressed is our hope

B. Some of us are not redeemed
   1. We can have a place among the redeemed
   2. The invitation has gone out — "Come"

29
Sunrise

II Timothy 1:7

1. Sunrise has a peculiar charm
2. Sick people can tell us much about sunrise
   a. They spend many restless nights longing for it
   b. Ps. 130:6 refers to those who watch for the morning
   c. Job 7:4 speaks of tossing to and fro
3. Jesus was an early riser — John 21:4; Mark 1:35
4. Paul's experience in a storm — Acts 27:29

I. Life Is Full of Storms and Conflict

A. They make us wish for the day
   1. Pain, sorrow, and uncertainty weary us
   2. They remind us of our need to be firmly anchored
      a. As we wait for the dawn and fleeing shadows
      b As we wait for the joy of the morning — Ps. 30:5b

B. Many are not sure of their sunrise

II. God Has Not Given the Spirit of Fear

A. Two great enemies of happiness
   1. Fear of past — rooted in guilt
      a. Of what we have sown — Gal. 6:7
   2. Fear of future — rooted in uncertainty
      a. Of standing before God and judgment

B. The Christian has no reason to fear death
   1. "Great day in the morning!" expresses hope

III. Another Sunrise Is Due Tomorrow

A. Promised at ascension — Acts 1:11

B. Promised by Paul — I Thess. 4

C. Promised by Peter — I Peter 5:4; and John — I John 3:2

D. Christians look for His coming — the sunrise
   1. 'Let us not weep as those without hope' — I Thess. 4:13

30

Escape from the Enemy

Hebrews 9:27

1. "Death row" is a sad situation
2. In one respect we are all on "Death Row"

I. Death Is a Common Enemy to All Living Things

A. Common to animals and humans alike
   1. Animals don't flirt with death
   2. Man has still to learn such respect
      a. He lives foolishly and dangerously
      b. He abuses his body and mind
   3. Death waits for all
      a. For the wise who live carefully
      b. For the strong who live vigorously
   4. Scripture warns — II Sam. 14:14; Rom. 5:12

B. It is a common appointment for all (text)

II. There Is an Escape from Death's Hold

A. Science has been unable to develop a cure for death

B. What man can't do, God has done
   1. First escapee was Jesus Christ
      a. Jesus escaped the hold of death, not the experience of death — Rom. 6:9
   2. Jesus delivers us from the hold of death — Heb. 2:14
   3. Jesus delivers us from the fear of death — Heb. 2:15

III. There Is a Death Worse Than Physical Death

A. Physical death is cessation of bodily functions

B. There is a worse possibility — Rev. 20:12-15

C. Those "in Christ" are delivered from the "second death"

31
Military Person

Hebrews 11:4

1. Story of Cain and Abel
   a. Abel died in earth's first human conflict
   b. Many have died in conflict
2. Text says Abel speaks to the living
3. Others who have died in conflict also speak to the living

I. Speaks of Virture of Human Freedom

A. Many question the rightness of wars
   1. Sometimes human freedom is at stake
   2. Sometimes we must get involved

B. It is hard to evaluate human freedom
   1. This makes it hard for some to pay the price
   2. Multitudes in bondage could tell us the value of freedom
   3. Patrick Henry, 1775: "Is life so dear, or peace so sweet, as to be purchased at the price of chains and slavery?"

C. When free men falter, freedom vanishes
   1. Danton, 1793: "Would we be free? If we no longer desire it, let us perish."
   2. Lincoln, 1863: ". . .from these honored dead we take increased devotion."

II. Speaks of Uncertainty of Life

A. Child goes out to play; young man goes off to war

B. Most ignored truth in life — James 4:13-17

III. Speaks of Importance of Life's Investments

A. There are many less worthy ways to die
   1. Many devote themselves to unworthy causes
   2. One woman died trying to retrieve her old car from a burning garage

B. Are we investing our lives in worthy causes?

C. One cause is more worthy than freedom — Acts 20:24

32

Tragedy

James 4:13-15

1. Three pressing burdens of a preacher

I. Bring a Word of Comfort to All

A. Two outstanding characteristics of God

1. His justness (justice)
   a. Moses' evaluation — Deut. 32:4
   b. Paul's statement — Gal. 6:7
   c. Jesus' revelation — Matt. 10:42
   d. Glimpse of judgment — Matt. 25:31-46
2. His great mercy
   a. Lord's own estimate — Jer. 3:12
   b. Publican's plea — Luke 18:13

II. Bring a Word of Understanding to the Young

A. The young have many questions about death

1. What has happened here?
   a. From human viewpoint — a tragedy
   b. Life and death can be illustrated by filling a jar with lake water and then pouring it back into the lake (Gen. 2:7)
2. Why has this happened?
   a. Generally speaking — Rom. 5:12
   b. Specifically, no one can say
   c. We trust in God's wisdom — Rom. 8:28
   d. We believe someday we will know all "whys"

III. Bring a Word of Concern to the Unsaved

A. Tragedy reminds us of our text — life is uncertain

B. This fact alone should cause concern

C. If one is saved, maybe the "why" will be answered

33

The Lord of the Bible

I. The Lord Is Good — Nah. 1:7a

A. This is assuming that God exists
1. Upon returning to earth the Russian cosmonaut said, "I did not see God up there."
2. God's presence can be seen everywhere
   a. Order, symmetry, law, intelligence, design
3. It is not the task of the church to prove God's existence

B. We are told that the Lord is good
1. He shows it by His concern for individuals
   a. You are one of 4 billion
   b. Yet the hairs of your head are numbered — Matt. 10:30
   c. The passing of the deceased is not unnoticed
2. He shows it by His willingness to forgive

II. The Lord Is a Stronghold — Nah. 1:7b

A. Death is a terrifying experience to most
1. Christians need not fear — I Cor. 15:55-57; Ps. 23
2. Nothing can separate us from God — John 10:29

B. The Lord is our storm cellar

III. The Lord Is Our Help — Ps. 40:17

A. In time of trouble
1. Life is full of trouble, and we will all face death in the end
2. In these times, the Lord is our help

IV. The Lord Is Our Strength — Ps. 27:1

A. To those who put trust in Him
1. Two men building houses — Matt. 7:24-27
2. Jesus is the Rock, the solid foundation

V. Final Word of Comfort

A. He knows those who trust Him — Job 19:25-26

34

Christ's Own

I. Christ Loves His Own to the End — John 13:1

A. John 13:1 is speaking of Christ's death

B. It also reveals His faithful nature — Heb. 13:5

1. The psalmist understood this — Ps. 23:4

C. It reveals that some are God's own

1. God's concern extends to all — II Peter 3:9
2. God's conditions must be met

D. Who qualifies as God's own?

1. Those who hear His voice — John 10:27
2. Those who obey His voice — John 14:15
3. Those who love Him — John 8:42

E. The relationship is one of love — Rom. 8:38-39

II. Christ Is with His Own to the End

A. This is intended as assurance of Christ's faithfulness

B. There is comfort here

1. Jesus was with the deceased in death
2. Jesus is with you right now
3. Jesus understands sorrow — Isa. 53:3

III. The End for Christ's Own Is Peaceful — Ps. 37:37

A. God's children are ready for death

1. Comforting words — John 14:1-7; Rev. 4:1-11
2. Their passing — Rev. 4:1-2

B. Last hours reveal the peace of the upright

1. Our brother prayed, "Lord, take me before morning."
2. There was no fear or panic but peaceful longing

35
Adventure of Death

1. Life is mysterious and beyond human understanding
2. The deceased enjoys a unique experience
   a. The cloud over his understanding has been removed
      (1) We see a poor reflection of the truth — I Cor. 13:12
   b. He has realized what Paul longed for — Phil. 3:12-14
3. This experience is not limited to a few
   a. Appointed to all — Heb. 9:27
   b. Imagine what we shall see

I. We Shall See the Angels of God

A. We should be glad to see them
   1. Keep us from wrong — Num.22:23; from harm — Matt. 18:10
   2. Usher us into heaven — Luke 16:22
   3. Watch over our bodies — Jude 9

II. We Shall See Saints of All Ages — I Thess. 4:13-18

A. Great men of the Bible — Moses, Peter, Paul, etc.
B. Family, friends, preachers, teachers

III. We Shall See Jesus

A. This is what every Christian desires
   1. Paul describes this longing — Rom. 8:22-23
   2. John Jasper, a Black preacher in Virginia during slavery, describes his longing: "Yes, mighty Angel, I does want dat crown, but first of all, I wants to find my Marse Jesus and fall down at His feet and thank Him for saving such a sinner as I was."
   3. We shall be changed — I John 3:2
B. Who will go to heaven?
   1. Those washed in blood — Rev. 7:14
   2. Those brought there by Jesus — John 14:3

36

What the Bible Says About Death

1. Peter thought of death as putting aside his "tabernacle" — II Peter 1:14
2. Paul spoke of death as a "departure" — II Tim. 4:6
3. Jesus simply referred to His death as "going away"
4. Jesus also said He was "being received"

I. Death in Scripture

A. There is no mention of the deaths of most of the apostles

B. Three things are given far more prominence

1. Duties and responsibilities of life
2. Rewards and punishment of eternity
3. How to be saved — the Atonement

II. Death as Putting Aside a "Tabernacle"

A. Like disrobing — taking off of garments

B. Like moving — joy of a new home

III. Death as a "Departure"

A. Israel departed from Egypt for a new home in Canaan

1. From bondage to freedom, from want to plenty

B. It's necessary to leave before we can arrive

IV. Death Is Ominous Only to the Unsaved

A. Man is destined to die and then to face judgment — Heb. 9:27

B. All can be at peace through God's provision — John 11:25

4-20-2020

- No Treaty With Israel Yet. Ezek. 38
- Two Witnesses. Enoch + Elijah
- No War of Gog and Magog Yet.
- First 42 months of Tribulation.
3. - Matt. 24:4-6 When the signs of His Coming.
The end is Not Yet. Beg. of Sorrows. The order of The "birth Pangs." The Abomination Matt. 24:21 - Daniel's "Time of Trouble.
- The Gospel Must go around The World MT. 24:14
- Outpouring of The Holy Spirit. Joel 2:28-31.
- Tribulation is "The Great and Terrible Day".
- Prov. 22:3 - Rev. 12:20
- Tribulation begins at The Rapture.

Be Faithful in kingdom giving. Perry Stone.org
Secrets of The 3rd Heaven 3595 Clvle. Tenn.
Prophetic Summit 37320